Help for Families of the Mentally Ill

Lloyd Ahlem

Publishing House
St. Louis

To Margaret Anderson
and
Reverend Clarence Anderson,
good friends and
faithful servants of God.

Copyright © 1983
Concordia Publishing House
3558 South Jefferson Avenue
St. Louis, MO 63118
Manufactured in the United States of America

Library of Congress Cataloging in Publication Data

Ahlem, Lloyd H.
    Help for families of the mentally ill.

    1. Mentally ill—Home care. 2. Mentally ill—
Religious life. I. Title.
RC439.5.A44   1983   248.8'6   82-14469
ISBN 0-570-08257-9

1 2 3 4 5 6 7 8 9 10 WP 92 91 90 89 88 87 86 85 84 83

Contents

Foreword

One of your loved ones is crying for help. And you, as you offer help, are crying too. Willing as you may be to stand by faithfully and lovingly, you are nevertheless on duty 24 hours a day, 7 days a week, in a setting not of your own choosing or making.

Apart from occasional visits and offers of assistance from others, the daily burden of care falls on you. It doesn't take long before your resources are drained and you cry for relief. If only someone understood your special needs. It's not that you want to abandon your station at the side of your loved one, but even those who care for patients grow weary and dispirited. The helper needs help, too.

This booklet, written by someone in a position similar to yours, is intended to offer you encouragement, support, and suggestions for outside assistance and understanding. It means to lift your eyes to your ever-present Helper and to open up avenues of communication with counselors and others in like circumstances.

Your cries for help have been heard.

—The Publisher

1
What Is a Mental Illness?

Mary is a 55-year-old supervisor of nurses in a convalescent hospital. She divorced her husband several years ago because of his drinking and abusive behavior. She began her present employment 30 years ago as a nurse's aid and has made steady progress. She has been chief nurse for three years, is quite well paid, but is in serious trouble.

Six months ago she was given additional duties that included fiscal planning and financial control of medical services. With much government regulation, high staff turnover, and declining financial strength of the hospital, pressure has been exerted upon her to get the place "shaped up." Taking her work home with her only complicated her life. She became cranky and irritable. She lived with two other singles, but her troublesomeness led to a breakup of housekeeping arrangements. Needing a home, she moved in with her son and family. But her irritability led to a family rift, and her daughter-in-law has ordered her to pack and get out.

The order to leave seemed to bring on a major breakdown in Mary's life. Her irritability has made her impossible to work with, and she has been given a medical leave—quite against her will. Now at home, with little to do and preoccupied with her troubles, she is deeply suspicious of anyone close to her. Her suspicious nature permeates all her waking hours. She believes that others are trying to go through her mail, that her food has been poisoned, and that her family is trying to put her away in an institution.

No amount of assurance or reasoning satisfies Mary. She disputes every effort to placate her feelings. Mealtime is a hassle. Her son's children bolt from the table and get out at the earliest possible moment. Her son is employed, and Mary is left at home with her daughter-in-law, who is chosen by circumstance to take care of Mary. She has been there for three months, and Mary's daughter-in-law is about to scream for help herself. Hence the eviction notice to Mary. But where can Mary go? Her funds are too limited for deluxe but available care. Public facilities are crowded, and care is questioned. Are both Mary and her family stuck with each other? Must the brunt be borne by the daughter-in-law?

The daughter-in-law, Jane, came for counsel in a mood of quiet desperation. Carefully controlling herself, she knew that she would lose self-control if no hope was in sight. She was in crisis. She felt that her marriage was at risk, because at some point she would have to get out of the house herself. Her guilt was rising, because she felt that she would be expected to cope with more than she could handle. Her morale was crashing, because Mary's sisters were old-timers. She envisioned Mary not getting any better for many years!

How many Janes are caring for difficult Marys? More than enough. For this Jane, *one* Mary is more than enough. The suffering experienced by a helper is sometimes greater than that of the person with the obvious problem. In Jane's case we worked out a solution that saved Jane first and then Mary. Making Jane the first priority was an interesting decision in itself, for seldom is that done. But we felt that if we lost Jane, we would very likely lose the whole family.

First we directed Mary and Jane to Mary's physician. He promptly consulted a geriatric psychiatrist. Medicine was prescribed to alleviate Mary's symptoms. This brought a small measure of peace to the household, but with it came considerable hope—an important ingredient at this moment.

Within two weeks a temporary hospital stay under psychiatric supervision was arranged for Mary. This was financially manageable and gave Jane a most appreciated

10

vacation. The attending physician watched Mary's every move and reaction for the first 24 hours of her stay. Staff followed up on his recommendations, with great care and sensitivity. After two weeks most of Mary's symptoms were alleviated. For three months doctor and family worked closely together. Her reentry to home and work was a delicate and difficult period, but a return to work was possible. The reentry was obviously not at the level of previous responsibility, but a simpler position on a part-time schedule was arranged.

At home, some of the struggles continued. Mary was still suspicious, but with less intensity. Jane learned what turned on Mary's symptoms and avoided these things. Jane's husband began to help with better understanding. Earlier, he would come home, sink into a chair and ignore as much as he could. Now he learned how to become part of the family's problem solving. But most important, Jane's needs were given a high priority. Escapes from constant supervision of Mary were provided. Since Mary's needs were lessened, her care was shared occasionally even by the children.

But what about people who do not get counsel or medical help and whose needs are not recognized? What about wives whose husbands do not become part of the solution? What about the Marys who do not respond to medicine and guidance and have no psychiatric consultation to guide them to reenter life? That is what this volume is about. It does not give an answer to every question, but it offers hope and encourages faith—to at least help a little. To achieve this goal, it deals with the nature of illness, the nature of healing and recovery, and help for desperate helpers.

Is there specific Biblical aid and comfort for the Janes and Marys in their special problems? What in a valid, Christian system of belief applies to them?

There is a Christian way and style of coping also for them. It may not always be a formula to be followed. Yet it is specific enough to be comprehended and believed.

2
Defining
Mental Illness

The actions and thoughts of the mentally ill are a puzzle to most of us. Experts do not agree as to why the mind works so strangely. Most laymen are baffled by odd antics and disorganized thoughts of the disturbed.

Perhaps we can establish a helpful point of view. If we could view the world as an ill person seems to view it, we may get some insight. Try to put yourself in his place. Remember that, as an ill person, you feel yourself threatened. You sense psychological danger and try to deal with it. But your efforts to relieve the stress have not been very effective. There has been a steady rise in intensity of the stress and in efforts to overcome it. Rational attempts to solve problems have been largely ineffective. As the tension mounts, less rational means of defense have been used more and more. When the battle seems lost, your mind makes its own moves. A break with reality results. You suspect that others will hurt you, or you think that you are someone else.

This break with reality is known as autocorrection. It serves the purpose of limiting one's awareness of threat. The mind involuntarily changes its view of the world and of itself. Instead of seeing oneself as a person about to be overwhelmed by problems, one changes one's view and sees oneself as a king, a Yankee center fielder, Napoleon, or some other imagined figure. Then one feels relieved and no longer threatened.

Obviously, if one thinks that he is Napoleon or some other such figure and proceeds to his job acting accordingly, he is going to have an interesting time of it. His associates will immediately see that he has lost his sense of reality. He becomes the butt of jokes or is unable to perform his duties. His symptoms relieve his perceived threat, but they create other problems that he is unable to solve. He is caught between his attempt to protect himself by odd behavior and the fact that he is so strange that his normal life is disrupted. He is in trouble if he protects himself, and he is in trouble if he does not. That is the dilemma of the mentally ill.

It is most important to recognize, that, from the viewpoint of the ill person, the symptoms manifested in the odd behavior *are very necessary*. Symptoms should *always* be regarded as necessary. To deprive an ill person of his symptoms again exposes him to threat and multiplies the psychological danger that he fears.

If we understand the reason why symptoms exist, the burden of caring for an ill person becomes more bearable. In the case of Mary, her extreme suspiciousness was at first seen as aggressiveness, designed to hurt those caring for her. Her family could not understand, at first, that Mary was not attacking them. Instead, she was desperately protecting herself. When her family finally discovered they were not under attack, their tension was relieved. Instead of trying to argue away Mary's allegations, they saved a lot of energy by simply accepting Mary's behavior and trying to help her. They did not allow needless conflict to get in the way. This is not easy, but it can be done, and when it is done, the problem is resolved to some extent.

Obviously not all illness appears in the form we have just described. The symptoms described are a particular form of break with reality. There are many kinds of symptoms, and any good text on abnormal psychology includes a complete description of the common categories. The American Psychiatric Association has published a manual of disorders commonly quoted in the textbooks.

What, then, is a good working definition of mental illness? Though there is considerable controversy in medical and psychological circles about the terms involved, consider the following:

1. Mental illness is a condition of the mind wherein the perceived stresses of life have caused the mind to adopt irrational behavior to protect itself from being overwhelmed.

2. We need to account also for the fact that some illnesses are not purely psychological. Some illnesses are the result of damage to or disease in nervous system cells and tissues. Thus illness can be defined as any disease of the nervous system, including primarily the brain, that disrupts behavior and limits normal functioning.

3. Some define illness in highly social terms. Within this definition an illness may be any chronic behavior that is disruptive to normal social behavior. Accordingly, an illness exists when one fails to function adequately in terms of usual social expectations. This is the most controversial definiton of the three and has the most troublesome implications for control and management. Sometimes the redemptive impact of God's people can be socially disruptive. More than one legitimate prophet has been seen as something other than a whole person.

The American Psychiatric Association lists three chief categories of illness, with a number of subheads under each. These three are:

1. Organic brain syndromes with brain pathology due, e.g., to fever, intoxication, tumors, arteriosclerosis, and accidents.

2. Psychogenic disorders. This group includes neuroses—serious maladaptive behavior; psychoses that involve serious personality disorganization and loss of accurate perception of reality and acute situational stresses, such as war or other disasters; and character disorders, such as deeply ingrained antisocial behaviors or lifelong patterns of undesirable behavior.

3. Mental retardation, which includes serious

14

impairment of intellectual functions resulting in very low IQ scores and serious learning problems. For our purposes in this booklet we will use terms other than those that define mental retardation, which is a special category requiring special treatment.

Many are unfamiliar with the precise meaning of terms used in describing abnormal behavior. They mix terms that have separate specific meanings and thereby often confuse others. Here are some terms that are often discussed and given definitions generally accepted by professionals.

Mental disorder: The whole range of mental disease, from mild to crippling, may be covered by this term, which refers to disturbance of mental functioning. The disturbance is serious enough to limit the victim's intellectual functioning or to upset his relationships with others. He is not able to function usefully in society and is a problem to himself. Thus the definiton is largely a social one. He is perceived to be in trouble by others.

Mental illness: Often used as synonymous with mental disorder. But its meaning is now usually limited to disorders involving brain pathology or severe personality disorganization. In most instances the illness is severely incapacitating.

Behavior disorder: Used especially in referring to problems that stem from faulty learning of society's expectations and not from brain pathology.

Insanity: Generally denotes serious mental disorder. It is unique in that it is a legal term and is seldom used in professional descriptions. It generally means the inability to manage one's affairs or to foresee the consequences of one's actions.

Emotional disturbance: Commonly used in

reference to serious problems of children. It refers to poor or inadequate personality organization. Children who are disturbed are easily upset, preoccupied, or enjoy some emotional satisfaction from inappropriate acts and expressions. They are unable to function satisfactorily in the school setting.

Mental disease: Formerly used to refer to persons with brain pathology but rarely used professionally today.

Psychopathology: Refers to the study and description of abnormal behavior.

Maladaptive behavior: Any behavior that has undesirable consequences for the individual, including a wide range from serious psychosis to unwise or unethical business or professional practices. Any behavior that complicates one's problems may be classified as maladaptive.

Psychosis: Disorder characterized by severe personality disorganization. It often results in loss of contact with reality.

Neuroses: Maladaptive responses that limit one's effectiveness in dealing with life's problems. Behavior is compelled strongly by perceived needs, but when the behavior is performed, other needs are not met or jeopardized, keeping the person in a state of constant irritation or anxiety.

A full classification scheme of mental disorders has been developed by the American Psychiatric Association and is published under the title, *Diagnostic and Statistical Manual of Mental Disorders.* This classification system is often cited and included in current texts on abnormal psychology.

3
The Helper's Cycle of Adjustment

Max was a retired social worker. He was reasonably well off—not rich and not hurting. Max's wife had died several years earlier, and he was resigned to living alone. In his early 60s he began to see that he might have some decades by himself. His children, two sons, lived across the country and only occasionally wrote or called. His was not a close family, and he did little to venture into wider social circles. Severe loneliness was both his choice and his fate.

As time passed, he became increasingly reclusive, withdrawing from church and community. He sent a taxi for his groceries and conducted his business by mail. Noting his absence, and wondering, a neighbor called at his home, making his way through its unmowed lawn. He rang the doorbell. After considerable time, Max answered. The visitor entered the house and was appalled.

Max had not washed or shaved in weeks. He had not eaten well. His house was unkempt. Uncashed retirement checks and bank statements cluttered his kitchen table. Rotting food raised a stench. The neighbor talked briefly to Max, but the conversation made little sense. Max's loss of contact with reality was obvious.

The neighbor located Max's son, who made arrangements to bring Max to his home, far across the country. The move, vacating the house, disposing of piles of junk, and changing environment and climate created more stress than Max's meager psychological resources could bear. He went into episodes of babbling, dressing oddly, and being present in his son's family doings at wrong times. He became the subject of every town gossip, and the son's family went into chaos.

While everyone talked about Max, the real victims were the son and family, especially the daughter-in-law, Georgene. She was trapped. No one talked of her predicament—only of Max and his odd ways. Max's son, Jim, escaped to work each day, blocking Max out of his mind. No such luxury for Georgene, Max was in her way every waking moment. The children spent more and more time at their friends' homes and suffered the reputation of having an "old nut" in their house.

If something like this has happened to you, you will recognize that your adjustment to it went through a number of phases. The first phase we will call "Wallop." It is the impact that almost drops you in your tracks. An unkempt Max moves in on you, and you are absolutely and totally stunned! A few get themselves absolutely and totally stoned to endure the wallop that has been delivered. For the first few days or hours, you cannot think rationally or comprehend what such a burden is going to mean. You respond like an emotionless robot, too stunned to feel, too smashed to cry, too over-whelmed to think. Max is dirty, irrational, intrusive, expensive and he is all yours! Wallop!

Unfortunately, while you are stunned, you have to make some decisions. Quickly, now, where will your guest sleep? What limits can you impose? Who pays for his keep? Can you get outside help? How can you curb the fussing of the kids? Can't Jim spend more time with Max? All these questions and more must be answered just to get through the routines of life in the first few days. Each question is one wallop after another.

In a few days the stunned feeling wears off. Your senses recover, but you wish that you could stay stunned—at least feel stunned occasionally. But with the brain working again, you realize fully that a burden has been dumped into your life and that you will live far differently than before—unless somebody else picks up the load you are bearing. Small chance of that! Now you fully comprehend the complications of your life. Morale crashes. Free time evaporates. Close friends abandon you. You skid emotionally into the pits for the next two months. Phase two is "Crash." Wallop was hard. At least the stunning blanked out some of the realities. But crash means heading downhill without brakes on your feelings.

During the crash phase you cry, hoping to get it out of your system. It does help a little, but when you are done you only cry again. For some weeks you slide into deeper emotional muck. You try to find a corner of the house where you can quietly gather your wits. But Max decides to take a walk with all his clothes off, and you have to decide whether to chase or to call the police. If you chased and caught him, what would you do with him? Explain to your neighbors that your father-in-law is taking up sunbathing? If you call the police, how will you explain to them or to your friends? Max is no criminal—just missing a few sensitivities.

Whether your problem is Max or someone else, you feel the impossibility of it all. You are caught in a no-win situation, and your feelings will not stop to bottom out. You have a Max-problem and a you-problem. You feel as if the load doubled because you are wondering whom to take care of now, yourself or Max.

At this point an important decision will be made—the most important one of all in getting your life and your Max problem under control. Psychologists call it the "fight-flight" decision. You will make a choice either to come up swinging, taking the matter as a challenge to be met—or to go down whimpering, running, ducking, avoiding, and escaping.

During earlier stages of your life you were probably conditioned to favor one alternative in the fight-flight choice. Your parents very likely demonstrated one or the other for you. Perhaps you had a dad who took every problem head-on, or perhaps one who shrank from every crisis. As a result of such examples and in your own developed style you tend to be a "fighter" or a "flighter." By the time you reach adulthood you will almost automatically make the flight-fight choice in each difficult problem. You are now making that choice in the crash phase with your Max problem.

If you possibly can, be a fighter! It is healthier for you, others take notice more easily, and you will more likely get help for both yourself and Max. Furthermore, the process of adjustment to your problem will probably be shortened. Those who try to avoid the problem extend the time of adjusting to it. They remain in doldrums too long and complicate other decisions that must be made while caring for Max.

The crash phase *will* end. Some days it will not seem so. But the human mind is resilient. It has bounce. So keep on struggling until you bottom out. "Cry until dry" is not a bad idea. Then you will be ready for a rebound.

While you are at the bottom of things you will need faith to get you through—faith that by God's grace you can be strong and resilient and that He knows your particular needs. For those reared in faith and with a store of precepts and assurances developed over the years, this will be a time of realization that religious training makes for strength. Earlier days of absorbing Scripture and feeding on pastoral admonitions are about to pay off.

Every fragment of God's truth is a resource. Every investment in learning and understanding the truths of God and His love for man is repaid with compound interest.

As a youngster I was raised in a Christian home and given many opportunities to memorize and comprehend basics of Christian faith. My home reinforced these truths with great love. Now every theological abstraction learned in early days is fiber in a tough fabric of faith. The result is a capacity to rebound with hope in the most grinding problems.

But I also find that more and more people are without the hope that enables one to rebound from crisis. A secular upbringing in optimistic humanism, rather than gutsy faith, fails to keep its promises at crisis time. If you are in this trap, do not hesitate to let the people of faith carry you. Your personal needs can be addressed with hope for your whole life. Your needs are your church's and your pastor's business.

Rebound will come. Rebound is the third phase of the problem, and it will come slowly and quietly. It will take hold of you if you let it. Rebound begins as your feelings bottom out. When your lowest ebb seems upon you, it will appear. It will continue until hope and the future become more probable than despair and past griefs. At first you will be tempted not to believe that rebound is possible. Your experience until now has been fairly convincing that you are in over your head. You will feel it coming and think it is a lie designed to torture you with false promise. But do not squash hope. It grows best with encouragement.

Consider the feelings of a lady who had been pushed into handling the affairs of a much older and mentally failing brother. After her life had been disorganized by these unwelcome responsibilities and her morale had been demolished, she was convinced that she would never escape from her trap. Her relatives had dumped a problem on her and then berated her for what resistance she offered.

But she had survived the wallop, had almost begun to despair, and at just about "give-up" time she wakened one morning with the thought that perhaps she need not quit hoping. But immediately she fought the thought, because it seemed only like a promise that would be snatched away, unfulfilled.

Her mixed feelings about hope lingered for several days. She wanted to hope so much. She feared hope so greatly. It was hard to hope! But her faith said "Hope is your gift and your promise from God!" So she accepted it as such. Her brother became a challenge more than a burden. Her hope became contagious. Her brother began to react with small smiles and thanks. They found a love for each other and reinforced each other's hope.

The family, however, had one more wound to inflict. "See! We told you it would work. We knew you should care

21

for brother!" they chided. Success with brother reinforced the rest of the family's self-righteous withdrawal. So there were some lonely moments and lack of support, but this wound was not mortal, and the helping sister grew and flourished, both emotionally and spiritually. Rebound and hope were polishing the promise, and the burden became a gift, as so often it does.

We have seen three phases of adjustment: Wallop, Crash, and Rebound. Now the final step—Win! My first teaching job came when I needed work. Any job looked good, but the teaching assignment was a special gift. I was to teach a class of mildly retarded children. I had majored in psychology, and so I imagined myself prepared. But prepared I was not. I knew nothing of curriculum, methods, laws, records, or professional protocol. I met my class with naive eagerness. Then came Wallop! More needs were bubbling in these kids than I could imagine. Some were truly dull of mind. But most were abused, disturbed, deprived, and raising Cain.

I went through all the phases, and rebound began about Christmas time. Vacation helped. I had learned much by trial and error, and now things were nearly under control. But the last stage, Win, was the best. Feeling some success, I decided to make education and the helping professions my career. What was once a wallop turned into a mission that lasted 25 years and now into work with seniors in retirement. Sometimes the burdens we are asked to pick up turn around to pick us up!

One of the finest examples of this turnaround, or Win phase of problem management, occurred during my days as a college president. I met a woman in Chicago with a son who was completely immune to elementary education. He suffered through eight years of failure, never learning to read the simplest material. His mother, burdened and bewildered, decided to do what no teacher could do—teach her son to read. But failure and fight became the order of the day. Mom and son could not get along.

The mother went to college and got a master's degree in

special education. Then she went to work on her son. She had to invent many new methods; her special training had mostly helped her learn what not to do. It took several years, but her son, a seriously effected dyslexic, learned to read. He eventually received his high school diploma and had a successful military experience.

Others learned of this mother's success and brought their problem children to her. Eventually a small school was formed. It grew, became accredited, and acquired a reputation for its success. We eventually provided facilities at our college for this school, and a number of our students got both vision and experience by helping to teach impaired youngsters. A wallop had become a mission—a genuine gift of grace. A depressed and discouraged mother became a practical missionary to others with similar needs.

So the cycle is complete when you sense that you will win. Let hope prevail and God's grace fill your needs.

4
When It Hurts to Help

Life for the helper is sometimes pure pain. The reasons it hurts are many. "I'm turning into a genuine grouch!" moaned a lady in her 50s. "We have come to the age where our kids are on their own and we thought we would be free for awhile. But Grandpa is our newest child. Feeding schedules, eating schedules, bedtime schedules, payment schedules—what can we do?"

Fortunately there are things that can be done. Most helpers need not stay buried in responsibilities. They can be free enough if a bit of resourcefulness is applied. One need not let personal life be inundated by demands of the ill or by the ones who made you most available to help. Two steps should be taken to get you enough personal liberty to make life tolerable again.

These steps go hand in hand and need to be repeated a number of times while caring for an ill person. The first step is to make a realistic assessment of the resources available to help you. Many people underestimate their access to such help. When they begin compiling a list of opportunities they are pleasantly surprised. Consider the following:

—Meals on Wheels, a service for the elderly and ill
—Volunteer nurses; free clinics
—Outpatient services of hospitals
—YMCAs and YWCAs
—Services offered by deacons and deaconesses
  of local churches

—Salvation Army; Red Cross
—Community colleges
—Individuals known to be helpful
—Local mental health organizations

This list is not nearly exhaustive. Every state and community has its own list and organization of community resources. I find that most people do not know about many available resources. Occasionally a helping organization cannot find enough people to serve and only want to be called. You may be doing someone a favor by requesting their assistance.

As much as possible, seek help through family and church. One of the great missions of the church is a healing ministry, and your problem may be a stimulus that allows Christians to serve meaningfully. Your family needs to bear a share of the responsibility, too, for its own spiritual health. Whatever your need, share it with someone. Do not hesitate to hunt. It is usually productive.

The second step involves a skill you need to learn, if you have not already done so. It is the skill of resolving conflict. Seeking help invokes conflict. To ask other family members to help may precipitate conflict. Getting yourself to ask for help involves a conflict within you that needs to be settled.

Perhaps you were awarded responsibility for someone ill because you were the loser in an argument about who was to care for that somene. Or maybe you are stuck with someone's care because you were one who avoided all conflict and gave in easily to pressing demands. You became a victim of your own peace-loving ways. Then you found that you had anything but peace. You are afraid that your request will reopen old conflicts.

Whatever help you seek, whether from other family members, friends, churches, or community agencies—it is going to involve some kind of conflict—conflict over responsibility for the problem, over time and schedules, over financial obligations, or even conflict within yourself about asking for assistance. So it is important to know how to resolve conflict in order to secure release from the problems getting you down. But getting into *some* kind of conflict will be your way to *some* kind of help.

If you find yourself the unwilling recipient of a care problem, you have very likely come out short in a what is called the "I Win—You Lose" solution. Somebody else won—you lost! You are stuck!

This is a classic and familiar method of conflict resolution. It is the method often used in the most difficult situations. Kids on playgrounds seldom negotiate their differences. When two get into a scrap, one wins, one loses. When a family squabbles over problems where the stakes are high, you find many "I Win—You Lose" solutions to problems just like kids. When care for an ill person is very necessary, someone will often precipitate an "I Win—You Lose" conflict to get the matter settled. It usually provides a quick solution and the case is closed. All but the loser, who must bear the problem, is released and perhaps satisfied.

Consistent losers are usually unhappy about their roles. Irritated and grumpy, they continue to bring up other issues and make complaints. This keeps the winners unhappy and the loser gets even. Or the loser symbolically acts out the battle he lost in another conflict that he can win and achieves a certain satisfaction.

If one accepts the role of loser too often, his future conflicts are more often resolved by the "I Love—You Win" method. This is a reversal of the "I Win—You Lose" solution. But the outcome differs only in the certainty of who loses. Losing is so habitual that the loser agrees in advance to lose. But in so doing, he is more deeply troubled and harder to rescue.

Some losers dig in their heels after a while and determine to have no more burden put upon them. This solves a problem for the new winner, but only means that someone else is a loser, with all the grudging that goes with it. The tables may have been turned, and there is a sort of fairness in it, but someone else's morale is now needlessly depressed.

The way to get out of the win-lose trap is to learn a method called "minimum loss-joint gain" conflict resolution. Several matters are important in adpting this method.

1. Recognize and do not deny your hurt in being in a difficult situation.

2. Do not expect to bear the burden totally yourself, and do not expect anyone else to bear it fully.

3. Insist to other parties in the conflict that your needs and feelings are honest and legitimate. Do not be phony with feelings, or manipulative. Honesty is especially important at this point. Do not lay guilt on anyone, and do not accept any guilt from anyone.

4. Put the facts out for inspection. What are the expenses? What time commitments are involved? Who has information? Who seems to be ducking away? Do not play hide and seek with information.

5. Clearly identify the joint gains that conflicting parties can achieve. Also identify the losses. Do a little psychological cost accounting. What behavior and what facets of the problem cost the most in morale? Get these facts on the table, too.

6. Finally, choose a solution that shares the burden. Account for each person's cost. Add up each person's gain. Then make a definite provisional try at a solution. Agree to talk again about the areas that continue to cause irritation. Now you are on your way. Nobody is a sole loser and justified in being grumpy. No one is a sole winner. No one need bear winner's guilt—a unique problem all its own!

Using as many resources as you can muster and constructively negotiating with all parties involved, you can come out from nearly impossible burdens and sense relief again. You must believe that you can keep at it productively. Self-pity and resignation will not work.

We can catalog many things that hurt you when you help a mentally ill person. These items may not be news to you, but to identify them will help you know that they are the usual matters—normal experiences in not-so-normal situations.

Loss of Time. Care for a disturbed person can require huge amounts of time. There may never be a moment when someone is not needed to supervise. On the other hand, many ill persons withdraw from all human contact and are therefore easily ignored. Illness ignored can lead to forgottenness. Is it any wonder that some helpers learn to value their patient's withdrawal more than his health? If a troubled person gets well, he does so by interacting and giving up his withdrawal. This may mean *much more* time for a helper's involvement. Thus the helper may unwittingly behave in ways that enforce the patient's withdrawal and preserve his own time controls.

If you assume care for an ill person, it is essential that you have a clear time priority for yourself. No caring person should be confined to work all the time. Some allow their time be taken by avoiding conflicts with those who should share the care. But conflict may be necessary to get quality time away from the ill individual. The caring person is entitled to it and should insist on it. Good stewardship of one's own psychological and spiritual resources is as necessary as caring for an ill individual. Help for the ill will be short-circuited if quality time is not scheduled. The entire family needs to understand this clearly.

Some families, by imposing win-lose solutions on a member designated to care for the ill one, will sacrifice the health of both the ill person and the helping person. This is not necessary, and every effort should be made to avoid such a situation. It may require a radical change in the way family problems are solved. If conflict is necessary, it will be worth it. Getting to "minimum loss—joint gain" solutions will avoid much grief for most family members.

It is also important to get *quality time* for the helpers—time when a healthy activity is going on, time in which good relationships are readily available and time when one is not so fatigued that activity is not very enjoyable. Occasional breaks as well as significant blocks of good time are helpful. No interminable stretches of work should ever be imposed.

Attitudes of Others. Misunderstanding of the mentally ill is common. Many are blamed for their difficulties. Sometimes they are treated as if they could stop acting the way they do by deciding to change. Relatives also get blamed or misunderstood. Families of the ill may be excluded from circles of friends. People who care for the ill do not rise in popularity or social prestige for their labors. Some may even think that they are contaminated by caring for a disturbed person!

These attitudes can be dealt with easily if experienced infrequently or not intensely. But with continual manifestation, morale gets chewed away. You become tired of trying to explain. You want to retaliate—get even! But such action only confirms the bigot's suspicions. Instead, try this:

Do not hide your ill patient. Discuss the matter of the disturbance openly. Insist on respect for the ill. They need specific love and assurance—not castigation. Let your burden become challenge and adventure as much as possible. Assess carefully whether or not you are adopting the poor attitudes expressed. You may be doing so unwittingly. Share your problems with others who are also caring for the ill. Bonds of common concern can be powerfully productive. Do not hesitate to pray off some anger or frustration. God does hear and care, and He seems to favor the oppressed. It certainly is better than unloading hostility on those who may be put off by your feelings.

My Own Sense of Loss. I have a minister friend whose wife became quickly senile the year he retired. Once a sharp-minded, vivacious lady, she became slow and simple, with many childish mannerisms. My friend told me that he was sure he could have cared for someone in this condition if it were not for the personal losses he felt—no more good evening conversations, no more little practical jokes, no more shared experiences and joys.

He felt as if he were going through a divorce—as if he were being rejected. His loving overtures to her were answered not with affection but with confusion. He was hurt and found himself tempted to hurt in return, but he recognized that impulse as foolish. What should he do? He was resourceful and found other female companionship. A widow living nearby welcomed his friendship. There were no improprieties, only honest recognition of need. When his wife eventually died, he continued his friendship with the widow. No, they never married. But they remained good friends.

A rule of thumb is helpful. When you experience loss, do not look for exact replacements. Instead, look for new experiences. Make new and different gains. Had the minister married the widow, he would have expected a replacement for his first wife. Instead, the widow provided a new relationship on nonmarital terms that permitted the loss to occur and a new and different resource to be discovered. No person can replace a lost relationship. It is unfair to both parties to try to replicate lost persons.

Little Reward for Efforts. I knew a missionary couple who had seven children. During their service in the Orient, one of the younger girls became quite agitated, then depressed. She behaved like a picky, troublesome child, creating a fuss at the most inopportune times. Visits with friends and church services were her favorite occasions. She tumbled from agitation to depression and secluded herself in her bedroom. Barely a teenager, she needed psychiatric care promptly. But little was available.

Her parents wrote to relatives in California indicating that they needed a resting place for their daughter. Could the relatives please help? Surely they could! But the severity of the problem was never explained. A childless aunt and uncle took her in, expecting satisfaction from being substitute parents. But fun it was not! Instead they acquired a cranky, agitated, depressed youngster, far from family and over-whelmed by her problem.

The aunt and uncle gave it a good try. In time the uncle withdrew, shunting the problem off on his wife. The aunt, now a fairly unwilling helper, found herself in the loser's role against her husband.

But the aunt went to work on matters. She got her husband's participation back—not without a stern confrontation or two. He soon saw his wife's plight and decided that one problem was better than two. He did not need an upset wife along with an ill niece. So they pulled together, trying to learn all they could about their niece's condition and what may have brought it about.

In a year the niece was much improved. Her depression abated, she had only sporadic sessions of agitation. It was time to return to her family. Arrangements were made, and the trip to the Orient was scheduled. The trip marked the line between illness and health. It was a new beginning for everyone involved, and it was anticipated with joy.

After the girl's return to her family, a short note arrived at the aunt and uncle's home. "Thanks for everything!" it said, with only a signature—and not another contact for several years.

The aunt and uncle quickly learned the thanklessness that goes with caring for such problems. They were dismayed and hurt. Where would the niece be if the relatives had not been available? In a mental hospital? In more trouble on the mission station? Such questions amplified the hurt. Is there no reward for long hours of supervision—no thanks for the money spent on food, doctors, and clothing? What compensation comes for struggling with depression and agitation, when you hardly know what you are doing with a relative dropped on your doorstep?

The fact is that people who recover seldom return to the scenes of their illness or recognize thankfully those who helped them. More often, illness is a difficult memory and

31

forgetfulness is part of the release. Only much later, with continued recovery and a more objective view, do patients return to thank their physicians and therapists. But if the helpers are looking for reward it will very likely come from faith that assures them that they have made a contribution to wholeness, not from thanks expressed. They will also learn to appreciate the insight they developed and a few important therapeutic skills they have learned.

The people who are helped turn away from the scene of their recovery. But they also see themselves, not their helpers, as the primary source of assistance. Whenever a counselee tells me that I was very helpful and that he could not have made it without me, I am a little worried. It tells me that the client has not yet seen the source of strength as being within himself. While it may massage my ego to hear such pleasing statements, I know that the therapy is still incomplete. His strength will be outside his reach when he needs it most.

So for the aunt and uncle who felt unrewarded for very dedicated efforts, the truth is that they may have been given the supreme compliment. They were no longer necessary. And who pays attention to those who are unnecessary!

I am going to digress a bit and give you a list of reactions that seem to typify those who recover. The reflections of people who have successfully come through their emotional difficulties are often different from the views of people who have yet to solve their problems. Those who are still struggling often point to someone or some idea outside themselves as their best hope for recovery. Those who have won their personal battles will often point to some aspect of their own ability or insight as the key to their solutions. The common descriptions of successful struggles include the following:

(1) *I saw myself differently.* One harried teenager, depressed and angry, eventually came out of his emotional pit with the discovered truth that "it was not all me!" He had tried to absorb and

32

internalize into himself the responsibility for every family stress and every failure of his church group and to atone for all his personal shortcomings. Under the preaching of a well-integrated and wholesome pastor from a fellowship other than his own, he discovered that he was working too hard at balancing moral and spiritual equations for the whole world. Then he declared that he had had enough! "I saw myself differently," said he, "with knowledge that God does the atoning and that I am really free." His anger and depression subsided remarkably.

(2) *I decided to cry later.* Most who recover have this comment to make. They come to a place where they put an end to their own catharsis. They stop crying and running mazes and blind alleys until fatigued. They have struggled until they hit bottom. Then they discovered that they can be better at the stewardship of tears, and with whatever grace and help is available they climb out of the pit—slowly at first, but they make it.

(3) *I quit hating.* No emotion is so expensive, so debilitating, so self-destructing as hate. It turns on the one who nourishes it and grinds him or her into gravel. But ending hate means finding a way to forgive. It is hard to do when the human instinct cries for vengeance and retribution. But when one can see the assailant as pitiable, lovable, and forgivable, the hate can cease. This is a personal enacting of a great theology—we forgive as we are forgiven, and our hate will cease. Then the self-destruction ends and recovery begins.

(4) *I found that I had to want to recover.* Therapists know that the symptoms of disturbed people become cherished possessions. Depression gets you sympathy, valet service, prayer, and much attention. To stop being depressed means

loss of these goodies as well as relationships. To some the loss is a price too high to pay. So they stay sick—trapped between threat of loss and destruction by their illness. But others, when asked, "Will you be made whole?" say, "Yes, I will." And they are on the road to recovery.

(5) *I got some good medical advice.* A gentleman I know struggled with anxiety for years. "I just feel squirrelly all the time" was his complaint. His problem? No great emotional trauma, no store of anger—just a developing case of hypoglycemia.

Seeing your doctor is your best first move.

Sense of Failure—Nothing Helps. Professionals who serve the mentally ill have had to adjust their expectations for success in treating the ill. Some came freshly graduated from training programs and were sure that they would help a great deal. Armed with the latest methods and with a good idea or two of their own, they launched into practice and waited for changes to occur in their clients. But if their experience was usual, they found very stubborn resistance to healing in many cases. Some healers get discouraged and change fields, some hang on, hoping less and less for success. An occasional one develops an approach that is especially artful, and he becomes a successful and gifted therapist.

Those who succeed are apparently in the minority. It is not necessarily the fault of the therapist. More likely it is the nature of the client and the nature of maladjustment. We were created with resiliences and rigidities. Our psychological construction was designed to proceed in an orderly and God-fearing way. That integrity stubbornly resists change. If a person has spent years growing and developing along certain lines, he does not ungrow or change quickly. His resistance to change, hence to therapy, will very likely be strong.

Consider the strength a gift. The strength that resists change also preserves health and maintains the mental balance in healthy people. The therapeutic task is not to break the strength of resistance to change, but rather to create conditions where changes can be made without too much threat to the ill one's integrity. He must choose his own changes!

If a lot of change occurs while you are serving the ill, you may be breaking the strength of the person. If the change is slow, steady, and chosen by the disturbed person, those changes will more likely be productive and useful. If you do not see great change, you might be thankful. If you see steady progress, perhaps you have a gift for assisting troubled people. If you are noting lots of changes and advertising the fact, you may be doing more harm than good.

At any rate, the feeling of failure by helpers is common.

You may be accused of not giving proper care by those who are very uncomfortable around ill people. But if you are meeting the basic needs of ill people for Godly love, care, and assurance, you are on the right track, and your patience and persistence will pay off. The visible signs are slow to come, but faith in your loving care will bring about good results.

Dirty Work. I counseled with a man whose wife had been injured in an auto accident. She was thrown from an open convertible and fractured her skull. Brain damage resulted. But marked personality changes had occurred. She was very short-tempered, raging at simple inconveniences. A pot of water that boiled more quickly than expected upset her so much that she threw the pot across the kitchen. Then she stamped out of the house to cool down. When she returned, she made no attempt to clean things up.

Her personal care deteriorated, too. She refused to bathe, body odor becoming highly offensive. Rather than washing, she wiped visible dirt off herself and her clothes. In a week after her release from the hospital she had made her home a dirty shambles.

Her intellect was also impaired in matters of good judgment. One day she leafed through a mail order catalog. Knowing that she could order articles by phone, she called the catalog office and bought merchandise worth thousands of dollars. Later, when the order arrived in a truck, she had no recollection of the purchase. She berated the driver and gathered all the stuff in her living room. Then she opened every package and left a room full of trash, with merchandise mixed and strewn everywhere. Her husband came home from work and was appalled.

The husband worked hard to support his family, but he could not control his wife's spending and conduct. Their daughter began staying with friends as much as possible. She was shattered and embarrassed. The husband tried to have his wife readmitted to the hospital. But after her discharge no insurance would cover costs, and hospitals were reluctant to accept her.

In the meantime, who cleans up both house and wife? Who takes time to help a daughter who does not understand and is so embarrassed that she can not discuss the matter? Work with people can be dirty work, especially when those who need help fight you all the way.

The solution is not easy. A state hospital took temporary custody. The wife felt rejected and humiliated by the placement. She escaped twice in the first week. But she was given medical help and was partially sedated. Her family visited her often, and in about six months time they began bringing her home. Constant instruction and supervision taught her basic self-care again. Her moods were controlled reasonably well by medication. Reduced agitation was the result. A clean woman could be lived with again.

But it hurts to see a loved one unkempt and resisting help. How can you help? Sometimes there is no other way than to just do it. Do it with as much love as can be mustered. But also persist in seeking aid. Ladies from the church took up visitation with the wife. The daughter began to see her life as a ministry, too, but she still needed to get away to express her grief and find some peace.

The wife died of a stroke about three years later. Father and daughter grieved at their loss but found they had developed a sensitivity to each other and to human needs in a way that they prized but hoped they would never have to learn again. They learned that faithful service has its own reward, however difficult it may be.

Fatigue. I know of no feeling that can destroy a good effort, distort a good mood, or shatter motivation like sheer tiredness. Work that is intrinsically valuable and stimulating becomes drudgery when we are tired. Fatigue cancels joy, dulls humor, and distorts vision.

Sometimes our fatigue is more a psychological response to frustration than weariness from well expended effort. In caring for mentally ill, the reason for fatigue is probably frustration more than physical effort. The solution to physical fatigue is rest—good sleep. It usually comes quite easily when we are physically tired. But the solution to the fatigue of frustration is more likely to be recreation, both mental and physical.

Fatigue narrows our perceptions. We are likely not to see the "big picture" in a fatigued state of mind. We are more likely to see our problem as the whole concern of our lives. Our spiritual and psychological boundaries are the boundaries of our problems. Furthermore, we resist those who try to tell us that we have narrowed our limits. We fend them off by saying, "You just do not understand the size of the problem." Some become so mired in their concerns that they believe that the entire world looks just like their problem.

Everyone is entitled to opportunity for reworking one's frame of mind. Some quality time away, with a specific enterprise that is different from the caring and concern you are involved in is vitally necessary. If you discover that you are resisting recreation and beginning to believe that you cannot afford to be away, it is a sure sign you need to be wrenched loose. At this point, fatigue has altered your self- and world-view so much that you are in danger yourself.

Plan your recreation so that both spiritual and physical resources are replenished. An inspirational retreat for a weekend will do wonders—perhaps a visit to see the sights in a new city, or a time of fellowship with people who are on the upbeat emotionally and spiritually in their lives. Physical fatigue can be slept away. Mental fatigue can be stimulated away.

Make specific plans for the next phase of your life. Plan not to be burdened forever. Develop a dream and begin to pursue it while you are encumbered with someone's care. The act of planning may be as refreshing as the dream itself.

Beware of self-pity. Our Lord admonished us, "Let not your heart be troubled." Most overburdened people have made a decision at some time to allow self-pity to take hold. But self-pity is like a narcotic. It gives a moment's relief, but it creates debilitating needs of its own.

Change or Loss of Priority. Illness occurs in family constellations and affects family dynamics. No one becomes ill all by himself. People become ill in a setting of relationships. Some of these relationships change with the onset of stress or illness. The stress that attends a family group has a way of focusing on the most vulnerable family member. The relational dynamics of the family can juggle the stress and focus it on a single member of the family.

Consider the following example: a family of four—mother, father, and two daughters. One daughter is brighter than the other. As a result, she is favored. The father loses his job and is emotionally crushed by the fact. He becomes difficult to live with and focuses his stress on the unfavored daughter, picking at her weakness and berating her ability. In time she is overwhelmed and becomes mentally ill, depressed, and agitated.

The father uses the daughter to relieve his own tension by berating her. But if she is to get well, she will learn to refuse her dad's picking at her. She will develop a sense of confidence that survives the stress placed upon her. But if she is successful, what happens to her dad? What does he do to secure relief? He has lost the one on whom he unloaded his excess tension. Her return to health may therefore be costly to

38

him—so costly that he will unknowingly resist her healing. If she gets well, he loses his stress-reducing mechanism.

In managing care for the ill, these dynamics should be considered and may require family therapy to get at the juggling of stresses taking place. To be effective in helping, an assessment of priorities is necessary. Whose stress gets top priority? In the case just mentioned, the daughter's recovery may be as much dependent on her father's finding employment as on her own self-image restoration. If father gets work, he will stop projecting tension upon his daughter. This will ease her recovery.

But a second kind of priority should be considered too. The person on whom the responsibility for care has been placed experiences changed priorities in personal value. If, in the illustration just given, the ill daughter returns to, or remains at, home, the caring one may get some of the same negative attention given the daughter. The caring one will find his or her needs reduced in importance—a kind of guilt by association. A devaluing of persons is sometimes experienced by those who do the caring.

If I am valued less because I do the caring, and if the time required for caring is great, it is easy to see that I am not going to be able to do many of my favorite things. Less attractive activities will replace the good things I want to do. This should not be allowed to happen completely. As in the case of dealing with loss of time, I must insist on some choice of activities. If that precipitates conflict, let it be useful conflict. Resistance may occur and should be expected, but no one should be overwhelmed by caring duties.

5
Spiritual Resources

Renewing Concepts of Persons. A legend about St. Francis of Assisi has stirred my imagination. In his younger days, St. Francis was known to require the very best things in life. Coming from a family of means, his tastes were for things elegant and refined. But one evening, while walking alone outside his village, he came upon a leper, dirty and covered with running sores. St. Francis was repulsed at the sight, but something within him commanded his compassion. He rushed to the leper, embracing him. In that moment the dirty, ill man became the figure of Christ. St. Francis was never the same again, and no longer did he yearn for elegance in his life. We recall the words of the Master, "As you did it to one of the least of these My brethren, you did it to Me" (Matthew 25:40 Revised Standard Version). This should be our view as we work with the mentally ill. A great spiritual resource in attending the ill is to allow for their transformation from undesirable burdens to images of Christ in our thinking. "Sheer delusion," you suggest? It is, unless one is transformed by the Holy Spirit.

"In this house I am the personal secretary, bedpan hauler, pill pusher, and exercise girl," lamented June, younger sister of a very depressed patient. June had been "selected" to oversee the affairs and personal care of her oldest sister. "Selected" meant being "fall guy." Since nobody else could be inconvenienced, June was made responsible. She reluctantly accepted her role after a miserable round-table discussion among family members as to who would take charge of the ailing sister. The discussion had deteriorated into a shuffling and dodging exercise in which dominant and loud members quickly voiced their reasons for not picking up the burden.

As is usually the case, we become identified with our occupations. We are what we do. We are salesmen, nurses, teachers, bankers. What we do has high significance for self-worth. We assign well-understood social and personal value to various occupations. We value doctors more than truck drivers, bankers more than cleaning ladies. June was assigned the occupation of personal caretaker for a sick and depressed sister. She had been a business-machine operator, but her company had been sold. She lost her job through no lack of competence of her own and was, therefore, available for the care of her sister. She was also available for a marked change of self-image!

The change from respected, employed business woman to bed-pan hauler brought severe self-devaluation. How do you explain your change of role at the ladies service clud? Nothing hurts so much as describing your new job and having friends gasp, "Oh, you poor dear!" If you really believe your personal worth is equal to your occupational value, you may, like June, be in trouble.

But being Christian can change all this. There is a beautiful example in John's and Luke's gospel. Jesus had gathered His followers and prepared to eat a meal with them. It was a somber occasion. Jesus was anticipating and discussing His death. But the disciples got into an argument over which of them was the greatest and entitled to the most deference. The argument may have included this, that the least important of them was to be foot-washer for the evening, a jab at anybody's self-esteem. But there was no more argument when Jesus laid aside His robe, donned a towel, and assumed the menial task Himself. He that was greatest among them was the servant of all—an example for all and for all time from the greatest of all.

Christians, too, have a choice to make. They can accept

the value-assessments that society establishes—or they can believe the value attributed by Biblical example. They can lift certain persons to high acceptance and prestige and relegate others to devalued personal worth just as society does. In the example cited, Jesus had little to do with values established by society. Servants were high on his scale. So also, in the helping role you can develop a sense of values based on divine information. And you can, like St. Francis, perceive your patients as being the image of Christ. When this change of values soaks into your consciousness, you can respond to your helping role in genuine joy. Your decision to serve will be bolstered by the Spirit Himself. The sight of you serving in joy, without bitter expression, will surprise a number of people. They will expect you to dislike what you have been stuck with, but you will be an inspiration to those who are facing similar problems.

Dealing with Negative Emotions. Mental health specialists identify serveral negative emotions as troublesome, even critical. Anger, fear, and guilt are feelings, that, if not well managed, destroy personality. If we indulge them they more surely become our undoing. With the frustrations of helping difficult people, anger comes spontaneously. It will rise up in us without our consent, and we will be tempted to let it linger and be nourished. It is therefore important that we acknowledge our feelings and accept them as normal and in need of management. It is necessary that we do something other than make a haven for negative feelings and feed them well.

We become angry when frustrated. Then, if we are told that we should not feel angry, we feel guilty—guilty about anger. Next comes a fear that we will feel too angry or too guilty. And that will make us even angrier. So a vicious circle develops, and we struggle to break the cycle. If we do not break it, it becomes our undoing. If we suppress all of it, we may deny our normal feelings, and that is not healthy either.

The critical point in the vicious circle comes just after the anger has erupted spontaneously and the temptation to nourish it into a grudge arises. Asaph, a psalmist, perhaps found himself in such a position. He found God's ear and unloaded his wretched feelings (Psalms 82—83). The beauty of these texts is that we learn that we *can* express our most negative attitudes and feelings to God in prayer and find it healthy to do so.

While conducting therapy with angry clients, I found two means that helped them unload their anguish. The first means was to have the client stuff his face in his pillow before sleeping and let God know fully and unequivocally how angry he was. Pray off the anger! You cannot unload the mental garbage on your spouse or family, but you *can* unload it on God. And if you do it before you learn to cherish it and manipulate others with it, you can dump it. This brakes the cycle without uncomfortably suppressing your honest feelings.

The second means follows the first. When a client had worked out his anguish fairly well, he was instructed to worship—especially to worship without self-reference, solely to enter into a frame of mind that beholds God and apprehends his loving nature and work. This lifts us out of the limited views we hold of our situations and puts us again into an eternal perspective. The effect is to diminish the overwhelming task we are involved in and put it back into God's order of things.

Another kind of negative emotion arises whenever we seriously care for troubled people. Psychologists call it pseudo guilt. This emotion is a guilt feeling that arises when we feel that we have failed or that we have performed our service poorly. We call it pseudo guilt because it may arise even when we have succeeded or performed well.

For example, a family I know struggled for years with their oldest son, an oversensitive and depressed high schooler. No relief came until he was in his 30s. After 10 years of grief they came to me, wondering what they had possibly done wrong. The lives of the parents and of the other children were of low morale, and feelings of failure dominated their conversation. They were determined to have me diagnose

43

their approach and tell them precisely and without equivocation where they had gone wrong.

We talked at length about how they felt. Then I suggested that we challenge their assumption that they had failed. They resisted strenuously, "Obviously we had failed," they insisted. "Are you making us out to be liars? How could anyone suggest otherwise? Just look at the boy! He is a mess, and we have had his care for 10 years!"

It took quite a while to get past their committed view that they had failed. But eventually I was able to show them that they had done everything they could, and did it right. They were, in fact, much more of a success than a failure. The problem was that the son still had severe symptoms, and by this fact they had measured themselves as failures, and guilt resulted. Their approach was not wrong—their success standard was wrong. They tied their right to feel free of guilt to their son's recovery—not to their good judgment and faithful care.

The ill son had sensed their guilt, too, and had learned to appear more ill than he was, in order to inflict his own anguish upon them. The family eventually learned to care without guilt, because none was justified or necessary. The ill boy also found no point in perpetuating his symptoms. The family's refusal to accept false guilt also stimulated the boy to take more responsibility for his own emotional status. Eventually he got well, finished college, and began a career. He is not the strongest person emotionally, but he is on his own, and the family is wonderfully relieved.

The point is, that we can feel falsely guilty. It may *not* be that we have failed. It may rather be that the standard by which we judge ourselves is in error. The standard for all Christian behavior is not necessarily success, but faithful service. Consider the apostle Paul in his efforts to nurture young churches. They were so full of problems that he was constantly struggling to keep them alive. They all eventually disappeared, having given him heartbreak. But Paul did not measure himself by the success of these churches, but by his faithfulness to his call. That is the difference. It is possible to do everything right and not have a good result to show. Should you feel guilty as a result? You will be tempted to do so. Instead, think twice. You may be able to unload a very unnecessary burden.

Koinonia. This Greek word for fellowship has taken on great meaning in the church in recent years. Today it means support and building of mutual trust. It means intercessory prayer for the burdens that any group member bears. My wife and I belong to such a group. We meet weekly for study and prayer. It is a place where members can share their joy and find help for their sorrows.

One couple is struggling with parents who suffer chronic illness and advanced age. The frustrations of keeping their mom and dad going while preventing very bad decisions by them is a daily concern. These parents are less than fully rational; they argue with each other and have many household misadventures, yet they refuse help until they have totally complicated their situation.

We pray for the couple who must care, and we share the burdens. The Christian life and experience was meant to do just that. The church was designed by God to gather people together for worship and to provide support for each other. There is no such thing as an isolated Christian success. There is no such person as a mature but lonely saint. There are no spiritually well-developed hermits. It is possible to be an isolated religious eccentric, but such folk are hardly helpful to the fellowship. They are always odd characters who seem to scratch where no one itches.

In bearing the burdens of the mentally ill, it is paramount that the caring family or person be vitally involved in a support group—a system of people pledged to pray and help as needed. The gathering together of believers for care and worship enjoys the special blessing of God. Those entrusted with care should never go it alone. They should seek to develop a relationship wherein several people can bear the load and offer intercessory prayer.

Let me close this treatise with a great promise from the apostle Paul: "Eye hath not seen, nor ear hear, neither have entered into the heart of man, the things which God hath prepared for them that love him" (1 Corinthians 2:9 KJV). We are the objects and recipients of His love and care. We are drawn into no task or experience in which He is not present with His love and promise of forgiveness. No human event escapes His understanding. He cares more about you and your burdens than you do. In Him you shall find rest for your soul. He will not leave you nor forget you. "Lo, I am with you alway." He knows who you are and has you in mind at all times.